By Steve Bray

Edited by Barrie Carson Turner
© 1993 International Music Publications Limited
Southend Road, Woodford Green, Essex IG8 8HN, England.

Reproducing this music in any form is illegal and forbidden by The Copyright, Designs and Patents Act 1988

Understanding Tablature	4
Introduction	5

SECTION 1 - The Basics

Note Chart	6
Guitar Strings	8
Picks and Plectrums	8
Pick Direction	8
Staccato Playing	8
Vibrato	8
The Semitone Bend	9
Tone Bends	10
The Pivot	10
The Squeeze	11

SECTION 2 - The Blue Scale, Pattern 1

The Notes of the Blues Scale	12
Riffs 1 - 30	13
Damping with the Thumb	14
Damping with the Pick and Fingernail	22
High Register Playing	29

SECTION 3 - The Blue Scale, Pattern 2

Riffs 31 - 50	30
The Pick and Finger Technique	36
High Register Playing	41

SECTION 4 - The Blue Scale, Pattern 3

Riffs 51 - 70	42

SECTION 5 - Blues Chords

The 12 Bar Riff	53
Chords and their Root Notes	55
Constructing Dominant - Type Chords	55
The Notes of the Blues Chords	56
Using Dominant 7th - Type Chords	58
Mixing up Dominant - Type Chords	59
Using Dominant 9th - Type Chords	60
The Minor Blues	61
Chord Substitution	62
Jazz/Blues Passing Chords	64

SECTION 6 - Chord Index

Chords with Notes Missing from the Formulas	71

UNDERSTANDING TABLATURE

The string bend fingerings I have suggested are not mandatory. If you prefer other fingerings, feel free to use them.

½ B

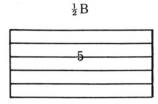

Bend string one semitone (one fret).

B

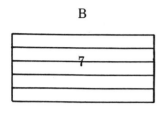

Bend string one tone (two frets).

R

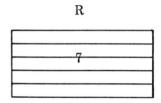

Release bend.

S

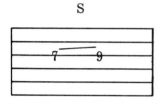

Slide from 7th - 9th fret.

PO

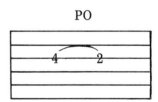

Pull-off.

HO

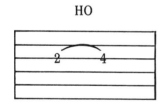

Hammer-on.

PO

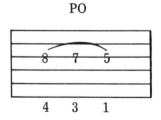

4 3 1

Double pull-off. Pull both notes off, starting with your 4th finger followed by your 3rd finger.

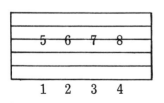

1 2 3 4

The numbers under the tablature are recommended left hand fingerings.

Note: Many guitar publications display chord patterns vertically, but since I believe this causes a delay in visualizing advanced chords, I have shown all chord patterns as they appear *as you look down* on the fretboard.

INTRODUCTION

One particular skill that never fails to impress anyone new to guitar playing is the ability to transcribe music - that is work out note for note – recorded solos quickly and accurately. To improve your skill at transcribing you must first increase your knowledge of the music you are listening to. For example, if you learn all the Blues riffs presented in this book you will recognize these riffs when someone else plays them.

The object of learning the Blues scale patterns is to give you a framework on which to base your own riffs. Also, this framework helps you to visualise the various positions of the riffs on the fretboard when you play in other keys.

There are some great Blues guitarists to listen to if you wish to study further once you have learnt the riffs and chords in this book. I particularly recommend *Blues Breakers* featuring Eric Clapton (Decca 1966) if you can manage to get a copy, or Gary Moore's album *Still Got the Blues* (Virgin 1990). Other Blues recording artists I recommend are: B B King, Robert Cray, Stevie Ray Vaughan, Johnny Winter, The Allman Brothers, Buddy Guy, Rory Gallagher, Albert King and T Bone Walker. There are lots more, but these are my favourites.

Listening is a very important part of your guitar improvement programme. By listening to experienced guitar players you will learn phrasing and timing.

Musical maturity takes time to develop. It consists of the ability to use chromaticism for tension, timing for flow, speed for excitement, and various other musical techniques which set the expert apart from the inexperienced player.

Your first efforts at improvising may be frustrating, since everyone has to go through the stages of trying to commit riffs to the subconscious mind in order to reduce thinking time. For example, novice guitarists play a riff then quickly think 'What shall I do next?' they make up their mind, and then play another riff. This thinking time may only be one or two seconds but it causes gaps in the musical flow. This is a normal stage to go through.

When you practise, first play through all the riffs you have learnt; then once you have recharged your memory, practise improvising with a backing track - or better still, another guitarist. Even professional guitar players run through a few riffs before a performance to warm up both mentally and physically.

It is not intended that the riffs in this book should always be played strictly as written; you might have to speed riffs up, play riffs slower, take a few notes off a riff, add a few notes onto a riff or completely change the timing of the riff. Improvisation means 'do it your way whatever materials are at hand'. The seventy riffs in this book will give you an invaluable insight into Blues lead guitar playing. Practise regularly and your progress is guaranteed.

SECTION 1 - The Basics

NOTE CHART

	NUT	1	2	3	4	5	6	7	8	9	10	11	12
E		F	F# Gb	G	G# Ab	A	A# Bb	B	C	C# Db	D	D# Eb	E
B		C	C# Db	D	D# Eb	E	F	F# Gb	G	G# Ab	A	A# Bb	B
G		G# Ab	A	A# Bb	B	C	C# Db	D	D# Eb	E	F	F# Gb	G
D		D# Eb	E	F	F# Gb	G	G# Ab	A	A# Bb	B	C	C# Db	D
A		A# Bb	B	C	C# Db	D	D# Eb	E	F	F# Gb	G	G# Ab	A
E		F	F# Gb	G	G# Ab	A	A# Bb	B	C	C# Db	D	D# Eb	E

Learning the notes on the guitar seems an impossible task when you first start, but with a logical approach it's fairly simple. The fact is, you can survive by just learning fourteen notes! For example, if you learn the main notes of the 6th (thickest) E string you can easily flatten or sharpen a note once you know the position of these seven main notes:

E	F	F# Gb	G	G# Ab	A	A# Bb	B	C	C# Db	D	D# Eb	E
	1		3		5		7	8		10		12

Next learn the seven main notes of the 5th (A) string:

A	A# Bb	B	C	C# Db	D	D# Eb	E	F	F# Gb	G	G# Ab	A
		2	3		5		7	8		10		12

The notes of the 6th string are identical to those of the 1st (thinnest) E string. So now you have three strings on which you can find notes; and you can use two of these strings to locate the other guitar notes:

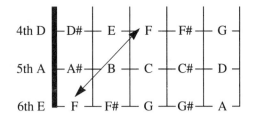

To locate notes on the 4th string use this pattern - it's the same all the way up the fretboard.

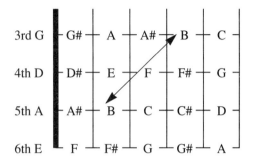

To locate any notes on the 3rd string use this pattern - this is also the same all the way up the fretboard.

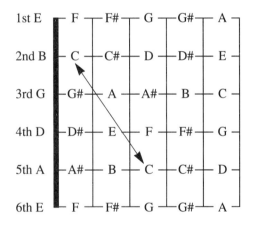

And finally, to locate any notes on the 2nd string use this pattern, also the same all the way up the fretboard.

You can use these patterns visually, or if you find this difficult, place your fingers on the patterns until you have worked out the notes.

Another way of learning the guitar notes is to practise exercises like this one I have mapped out for you, giving you all the G notes up to the 12th fret:

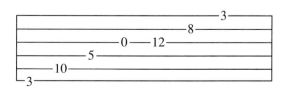

GUITAR STRINGS

The gauge of your strings is a personal thing. Gary Moore uses heavy strings, and the late Stevie Ray Vaughan sometimes used phenomenally-heavy strings, stating he had played with a 17 gauge (thin) E string. Thicker strings definitely have a better tone, but for anyone new to guitar playing I recommend an 8 or 9 gauge, particularly for bending strings. This is the gauge of your thinnest E string, the rest of the strings will be gauged in ratio with this string.

PICKS AND PLECTRUMS

The Americans often seem to use the term 'pick', but British players usually say 'plectrum'. Some players roughen up their plectrum with a nail-file or matchbox – this causes the plectrum to produce a scraping sound as the strings are played. Again the choice is yours. There are numerous plectrum types available. I have met players who swear that their choice of plectrum makes them faster, or play better in some way!

PICK DIRECTION

To ensure that you approach the riffs in the easiest possible way I have mapped out the picking direction of each riff. On some of the riffs I have taken you step-by-step through the techniques, indicating the picking as I describe the best approach to tackling the riff; but on the easier riffs simply follow the picking as shown under the tablature:
D = Down (towards the floor)
U = Up (towards the ceiling)
e.g. - U-D-U   D-U-D

STACCATO PLAYING

Staccato means 'in a short, sharp manner'. To make a staccato sound, play the note, then using your plectrum, immediately stop the string sounding. Sometimes Blues guitarists use a succession of 'up' picks to play staccato-type riffs, scraping their plectrum up the strings.

VIBRATO

Vibrato is a technique that most guitarists use at one time or another. It is a personal thing, and the frequency with which you use it can only be *your* choice, but obviously if you are copying a solo exactly then you should copy the vibrato. One thing that beginners often do is to move their fingers from side to side, only to realize nothing is happening. They may have watched guitar players on TV or at concerts and noticed vibrato is being used, but don't actually manage to copy the vibrato successfully. They usually end up with a similar finger movement but the guitar strings hardly move.

Look at these examples:

The Novice Vibrato
The finger moves from side to side along the string with hardly any fluctuation in pitch.

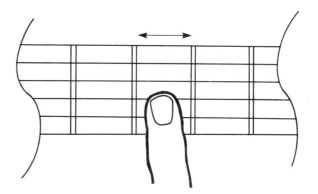

The Real Vibrato
The guitar string moves up and down evenly.

The speed of the vibrato and the degree of the vibrato movement is up to you. Any riff that finishes on a long note may sound good with vibrato. If you are having difficulty applying vibrato, then try the pivot technique that I have explained for tone bends.

THE SEMITONE BEND

Most of the great Blues players use the semitone bend. On your tablature this technique will be called the ½ bend. It involves pulling or pushing the 2nd note of the Blues scale, i.e. the C, until it rises one semitone to C#, then immediately returning your plectrum to rest against the string to cut out the sound, before releasing the bend silently. Most guitarists 'pull' the semitone bend, but some do prefer to 'push' the bend. Whichever way you choose, make sure that on the thickest E string you only *pull* the bend and on the thinnest E string you *push* the bend, otherwise these strings may slip over the edge of your fretboard.

Pushing the ½ Bend

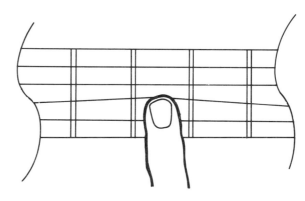

Pulling the ½ Bend

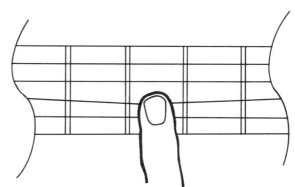

TONE BENDS

Tone bends are usually played by pushing the string upwards (towards the ceiling). There are guitar players who pull bends down a tone but this is not the most practical way to bend strings (it limits vibrato and makes some riffs unplayable). The best way to learn string bending is first to listen to the pitch you are trying to reach. For example, if you are bending upwards to an E, play the E first, then push the D up until you can match the E sound.

Vibrato on string bending is definitely one of the most difficult lead guitar skills to develop. I have planned out two approaches to this elusive technique. The first approach is entitled 'The Pivot'.

THE PIVOT

This technique involves keeping the web of your hand (between the thumb and 1st finger) tight against the guitar neck, but leaving a gap between your 4th (smallest) finger and the guitar neck. Place your thumb over the top of the guitar neck for extra stability. Make sure your fingers are approaching the string at approximately 45° so that when the string bend is played the fingers will finish in a near vertical position. The technique involves keeping the fingers absolutely rigid and rocking the full hand to close the gap indicated in the diagram. You can use the weight of your guitar to help produce this rocking action which in turn produces the vibrato. This is the best approach for anyone new to bending strings. For this technique I also recommend using your 1st *and* 2nd fingers. Notice how the 1st finger is one fret below the 2nd finger. This is because it is there to help stop the bend from slipping and to give you more push. When string bending, make sure your fingers don't go underneath any of the other guitar strings, instead let these strings roll under the fingertips to rest on top of the string you are bending.

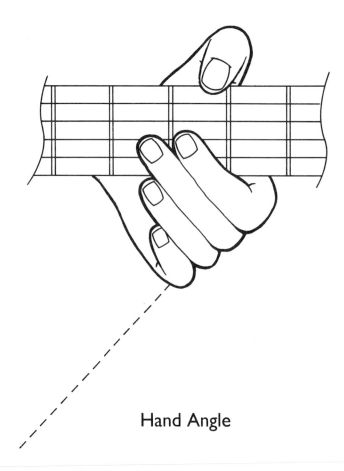

Hand Angle

THE SQUEEZE

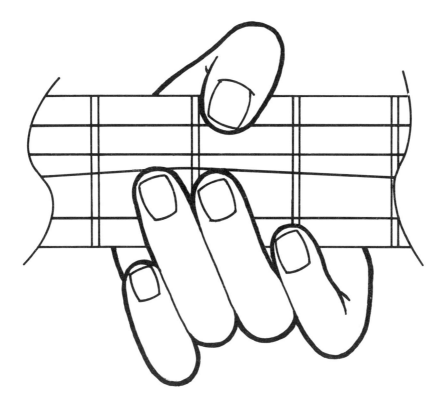

This is by far the most difficult bend to play and one that requires a considerable amount of skill. Once you have developed this technique, however, you will be able to produce very fast, fine vibrato on your string bends - a skill which only the best lead guitar players achieve.

This technique involves your hand being close to the guitar neck (with no gap at all) with your thumb positioned directly over the 2nd & 3rd fingers. The object is to squeeze your thumb and finger close together so that they push the bend into place. Once you have reached the required pitch, vibrate your 2nd & 3rd fingers rapidly, moving the string only about 1mm each way. Don't be surprised if your first attempts achieve nothing. This technique takes a lot of hard work - some guitarists practise for two years before they make any real progress. For a good example of an expert player bending strings, listen to Gary Moore's *Parisienne Walkways* (MCA 1978).

Most guitarists do not use tone bends on the covered strings, (E, A & D). Apart from being heavy in gauge, these strings do not have the same tone as the three plain strings. Also, it would not be possible to push the E & A strings up a full tone without the strings going over the edge of most guitar fretboards.

So to summarize, with the *pivot*, it's the hand that produces the vibrato; but with the *squeeze* it's the fingers that move. It is not necessary to apply either method to the semitone bend, since this bend only requires slight effort to reach pitch, also vibrato is not usually involved.

SECTION 2 - The Blue Scale, Pattern 1

THE NOTES OF THE BLUES SCALE

Technically, the Blues scale is the minor pentatonic scale with an added ♭5, (E♭) but where possible I have written E♭ as D# because it is easier to sight-read (as there are already three sharps in the key of A).

The notes of the Blues scale in A are: A C D E♭ E G

The main pattern of the Blues scale is based on the notes of the 6th (thickest) string. The key note, also known as the root note, is the very first note of this scale - A.

The Blues scale in A

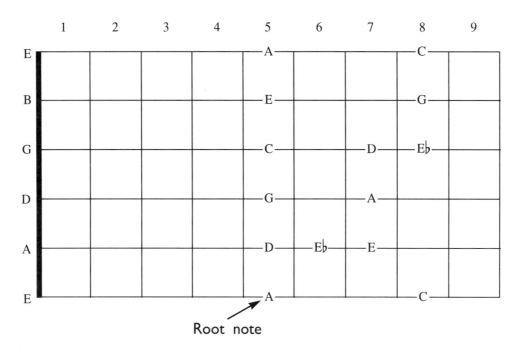

Root note

This is the most commonly-used pattern of the Blues scale. There are only six notes in the scale but these six notes are repeated twice (two octaves) with the first two notes of the scale repeated a third time on the (thinnest) E string. This gives us blue notes on all six strings.
The riffs in this book incorporate many pull-offs, slides and hammer-ons. These techniques add excitement, flavour and skill to your Blues soloing.

Note:
The Blues scale is the minor pentatonic scale but with the flattened 5th added.

The A minor pentatonic scale
| 1 | ♭3 | 4 | 5 | ♭7 |
| A | C | D | E | G |

The A Blues scale
| 1 | ♭3 | 4 | ♭5 | 5 | ♭7 |
| A | C | D | E♭ | E | G |

RIFF 1

This is simply the Blues scale played to the first A note of the second octave. Try using only 'up' picks with your plectrum, and play the notes staccato. Also, try roughening your plectrum with a nail-file or matchbox, for that 'pick/scrape' sound.

Play the second note (C) as a semitone bend. Pull the note with your 4th finger until it rises in pitch to C# then immediately stop the sound with your plectrum. This semitone bend, C - C#, is one of the most frequently-used standard Blues techniques.

This riff can also be played by using different fingering, and transferring the semitone bend to the 5th string 3rd fret.

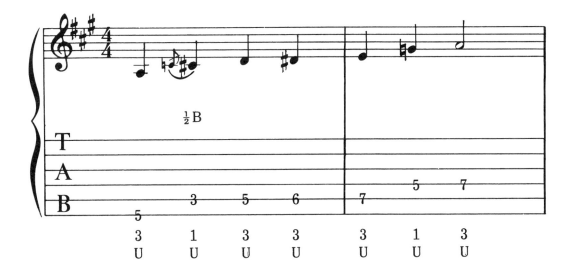

RIFF 2

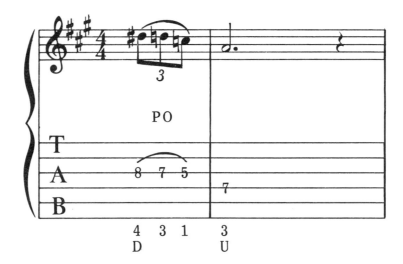

This is one of the trickiest riffs to play successfully. First place all three fingers on the fretboard, and while pressing down fairly hard pull off the 4th finger, flicking the string in a downward direction (towards the floor).

Then pull off the 3rd finger (giving you the double pull-off). Finally, finish the riff with the last note - A. Remember only to use the plectrum once on the double pull-off. This pull-off action will produce all three notes.

Finish with vibrato on the last note, making sure the string moves about 2mm each way for a good, well-rounded sound.

RIFF 3

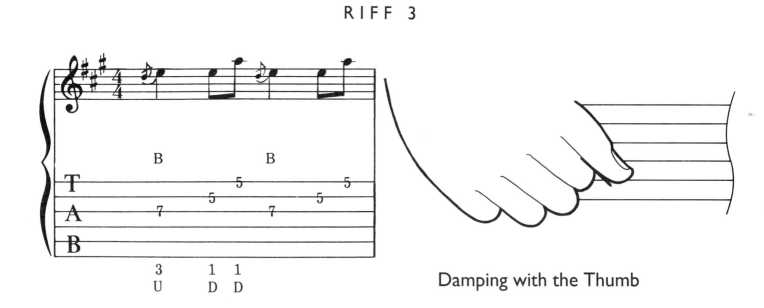

Damping with the Thumb

Play the bend with your 3rd finger. If you have difficulty reaching the E, use your 2nd finger to help by pressing it against the fret below (6th fret same string). Play the E & A with a barre, placing the 1st finger over both notes. Try repeating this riff quickly, four times.

A common technique used with this riff is to play the bend and immediately drop the right-hand thumb onto the string to cut out the sound. Then release the bend and finish on the E & A.

RIFF 4

This riff is fairly easy to play. Some players use their 3rd finger on the bend. This is up to you! This frequently-played riff is often repeated for several bars. Make sure the bend is still raised when you play the second (G) note, then immediately bring the bend down. Pick the riff with an 'up' pick on the bend and a 'down' pick on the 2nd string. This keeps the picking action on the inside of the strings which is far easier and safer than playing on the outside of the two strings.

RIFF 5

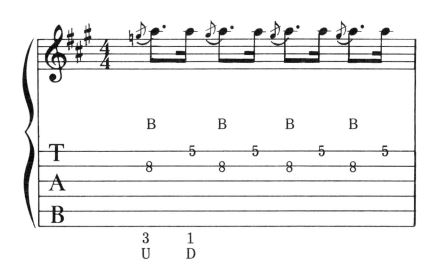

This riff is similar to Riff 4. Play both notes on the inside of the strings using an 'up' pick then a 'down' pick for the second note. Try cutting out the bend with the right-hand thumb as in Riff 3. If you find the bend difficult to perform, your 2nd finger placed on the 7th fret will help you. Try repeating this riff very quickly, eight times.

RIFF 6

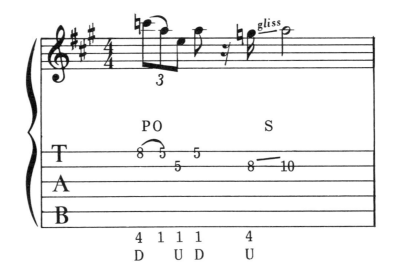

Start Riff 6 with a barre on the E & B strings placed at the 5th fret, using your 1st finger. Play the C with a 'down' pick to produce the 4th finger pull-off, then an 'up' pick for the E, 2nd string. Use another 'down' pick for the A, 1st string, and finally an 'up' pick to finish with the slide, using your 4th finger. Add a gentle vibrato to the last (A) note.

RIFF 7

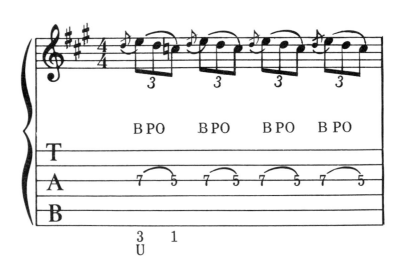

Another very common technique is used with this riff. Push the bend up using both the 3rd & 1st fingers. Bring down the bend and pull off the 3rd finger in one motion - only use the plectrum once to produce the three notes. This riff is sometimes repeated several times, finishing with the bend. If you finish with the bend, use vibrato on the string while the bend is raised, gradually letting the sound fade out naturally.

RIFF 8

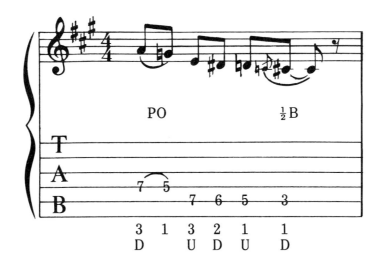

This riff sounds great when played quickly. Play the pull-off with a 'down' pick, then on the 5th string pick 'up-down-up' and finish with the semitone bend using a 'down' pick. Don't forget to cut out the bend with your plectrum as soon as you reach the C#, then release the string silently.

RIFF 9

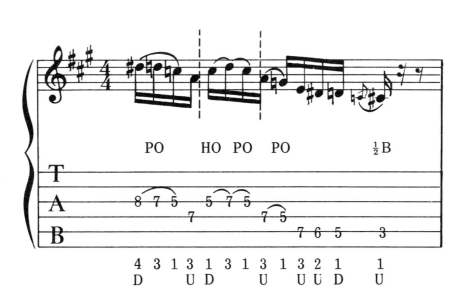

Notice Riff 9 actually starts with Riff 2, followed by different material forming a middle section (inside dotted lines) before the riff finishes with Riff 8. This is a good example of joining smaller riffs together to produce a longer riff. When playing the middle section keep your 1st finger on the 3rd string 5th fret for the hammer-on and pull-off.

RIFF 10

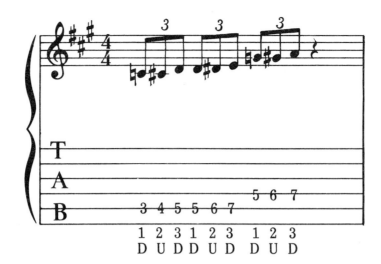

This is probably the easiest riff to play so far. The sequence should have a triplet feel (in groups of three). Pick 'down-up-down' as you play each set of three notes. Notice this riff contains chromatic notes (notes not from the scale). Technically, a chromatic run is a run of semitones (one-fret movements). Use a gentle vibrato on the last note (A).

RIFF 11

This riff is not as easy as you may think. For an inexperienced player the bend will be difficult, but there are two things which will help you: either cut the bend short by stopping the sound with your plectrum, as with the semitone bends we have played; or hold the bend on with a vibrato. Try different types of vibrato.

RIFF 12

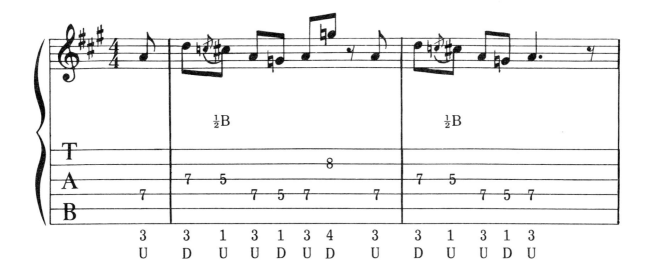

This is another fairly long Blues riff. Play the first note with an 'up' pick then roll the 3rd finger down onto the 3rd string for the D note with a 'down' pick. Play the semitone bend with an 'up' pick, and by using another 'up' pick cut out the sound with your plectrum. Play the 4th string notes 'up-down-up'. This prepares you to skip the 3rd string for the G note 2nd string played with a 'down' pick. Repeat the picking sequence, finishing with vibrato on the A note 4th string.

RIFF 13

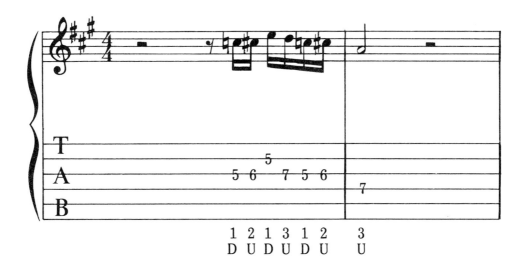

This is a fairly easy riff. Twist your plectrum to slice across both strings when playing the last two notes. This is technically called 'sweep picking' - taking both strings with one pick direction. Finish with vibrato.

RIFF 14

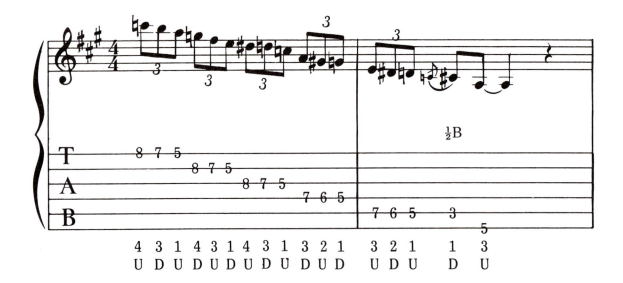

This riff sounds impressive when played quickly. Notice again the use of chromatic notes and the semitone bend. Be careful not to push the 6th string over the edge of your fretboard if you apply vibrato to the last note.

RIFF 15

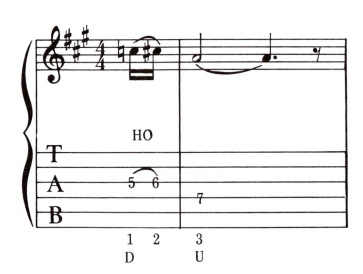

This is a very easy riff to play well. The first two notes are actually the notes used in the semitone bend C - C#, but in this riff just play the notes straight. Finish with vibrato on the A, but don't keep your 1st finger in place - this will limit your vibrato.

RIFF 16

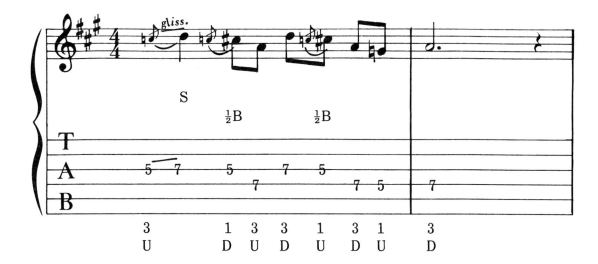

Play the slide with an 'up' pick followed by the 1/2 bend with a 'down' pick. Don't use your plectrum to stop the 1/2 bend sounding unless you play the riff very slowly. Use your 3rd finger to barre the 4th & 3rd strings for the A & D notes, using an 'up' and then a 'down' pick. Finish with U-D-U-D and vibrato on the final A.

RIFF 17

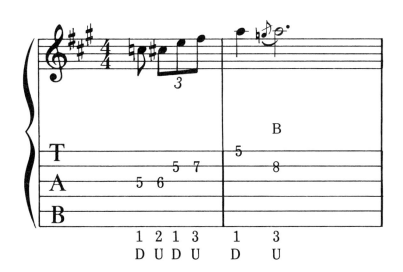

The first part of this riff is straightforward - it's the bend that is the difficult part. Try using your 3rd finger on the 8th fret 2nd string and your 2nd finger on the same string 7th fret to support the bend and prevent the string slipping. Try to play the riff quickly, and finish the bend with a fast, fine vibrato - only moving the string about 1mm in each direction.
Don't release the bend until the sound fades out.

RIFF 18

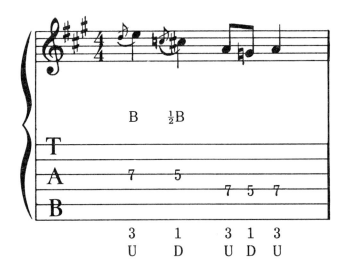

Play the tone bend with an 'up' pick then stop the bend with a further 'up' pick once the pitch reaches E. Release the bend silently before playing the ½ bend with a 'down' pick. Finish the riff with U-D-U, picking on your 4th string.

RIFF 19

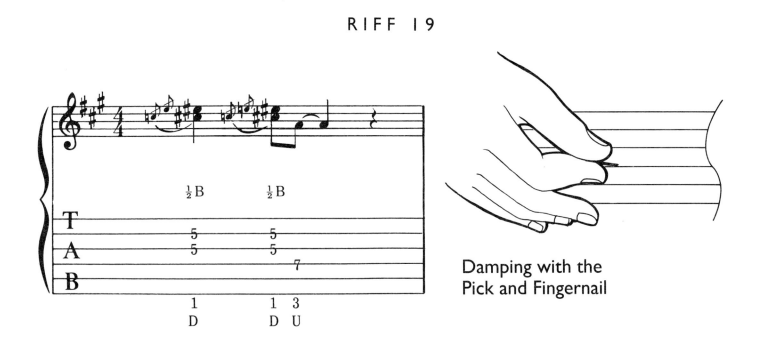

Damping with the Pick and Fingernail

This riff is a very common 'standard idea'. Play the two 5th fret notes (C & E) with your 1st finger, using the ½ bend technique, but pulling both strings down together using one 'down' stroke of your plectrum. Stop the 3rd string sounding with your plectrum as usual, but also stop the 2nd string at the same time by using the right-hand index fingernail. Repeat the double semitone bend then finish with vibrato on the A.

RIFF 20

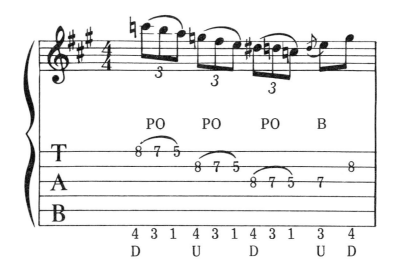

This is not an easy riff to play. Use the double pull-off technique from Riff 2, but remember only to pick each set of pull-off notes once. Pick D-U-D. Play the bend with another 'up' pick then play the final G with a 'down' pick. Keep the bend up while you play the G.

RIFF 21

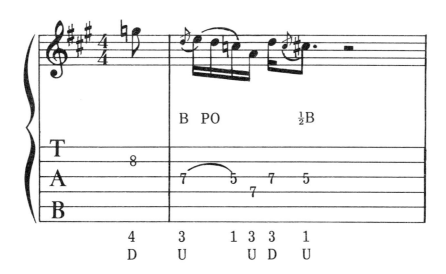

This riff should not be too difficult. Play the first note with a 'down' pick then use an 'up' pick for the combined bend pull-off technique (see Riff 7). Use an 'up' pick then a 'down' pick on the two 7th fret notes (A & D). Finish with the $\frac{1}{2}$ bend. Don't forget to roll your 3rd finger down for the A & D notes (7th fret).

RIFF 22

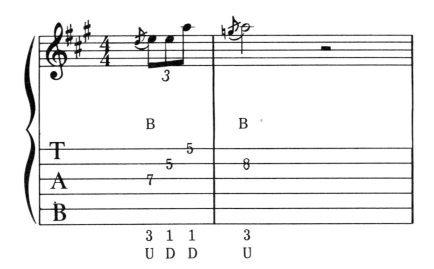

This riff is an extension of Riff 3. Play the last bend with an 'up' pick. Try to use a fast, fine vibrato. Alternatively you could try releasing the bend very slowly back down to G, fading out to prepare for another riff.

RIFF 23

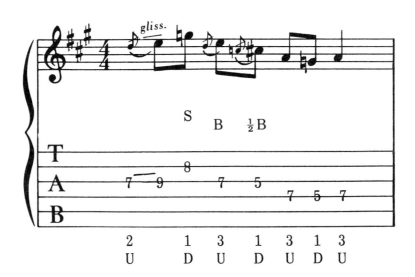

Use an 'up' pick for the opening slide then a 'down' pick for the G. Play the tone bend with an 'up' pick, stopping the sound with your plectrum once the bend reaches the E. Play the 1/2 bend with a 'down' pick, finishing the riff with U-D-U on the three 4th string notes. Play the final A with vibrato.

RIFF 24

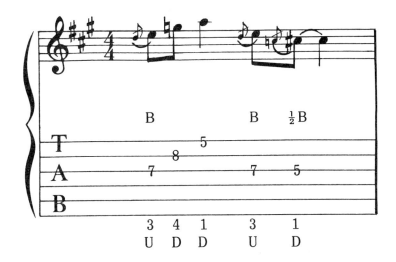

This riff should be straightforward to play as we have already covered all relevant techniques. Play the first bend with an 'up' pick, followed by the G & A notes with two 'down' picks. Play the last two bends with an 'up' pick then a 'down' pick, stopping both notes with your plectrum once bending pitch is reached.

RIFF 25

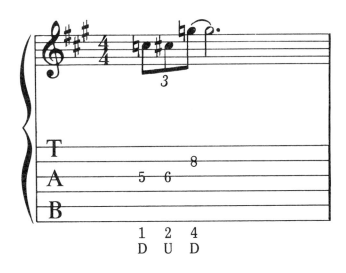

This riff - used frequently by many guitarists - should give you no difficulty. Pick D-U-D, and finish with vibrato.

RIFF 26

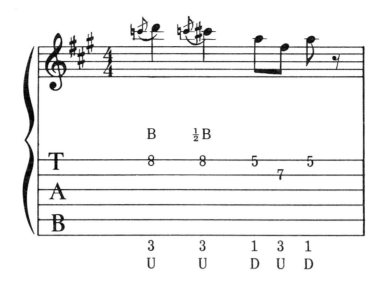

The technique needed for this riff is not easy to attain. The best approach is to first familiarize yourself with the sound of the two bends. To do this, begin by playing the D, 1st string 10th fret, and the C#, 1st string 9th fret separately. Once you feel you know this sound, take the first bend up a tone to D. Stop the sound with your plectrum and release the bend silently. Then take the second bend up a semitone to C#. Stop the sound with your plectrum and release the bend silently.

RIFF 27

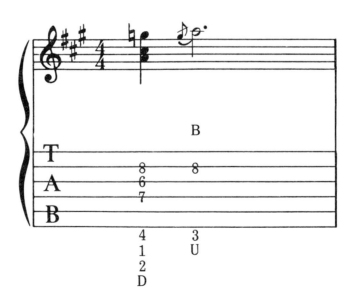

This riff contains a string rake over part of an A7 arpeggio. Place your three left-hand fingers in position for the rake. Then slice across the three strings with one downward sweep of your plectrum, immediately releasing the pressure off your left-hand fingers to produce a muted sound. Finish by playing the bend with an 'up' pick, using a fast, fine vibrato.

RIFF 28

This riff involves using double-bend techniques. Position your 3rd & 2nd fingers for the first double bend. Use a 'down' pick, taking both strings up one tone, then immediately release the strings so the sound of the release is heard. Finally, finish with the double $1/2$ bend and the final A as in Riff 19.

RIFF 29

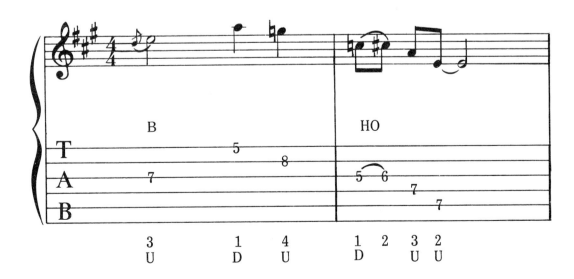

This riff is fairly straightforward. Most beginners will use their 3rd finger on both of the last two notes (A & E) resulting in a very short A note; but by using the 3rd & 2nd fingers you can let both notes ring on together.

RIFF 30

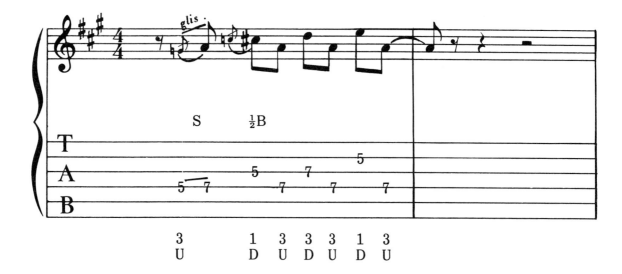

This riff contains a string skip, but other than that there should be no problem. Don't forget to roll the 3rd finger down for the A & D notes 7th fret, and finish with vibrato.

With these thirty riffs we have covered most of the standard Blues techniques used in the main pattern of the Blues scale. If you want to play these riffs in other keys, follow this example:

Let's begin with the key of C. So, find the C note on the 6th string and play your scale in that position (the scale of C). Then, all you have to do is to remember how the position of each riff is related to the scale in A and so relate each riff to the new key.

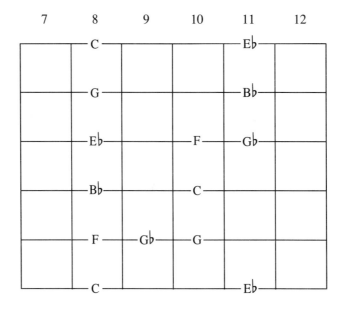

HIGH REGISTER PLAYING

29

The Blues scale pattern and each riff may also be played twelve frets higher, at the 17th fret. Some of the riffs may be very difficult to play in this position, depending on your guitar, but you still need to be capable of playing in this higher register.

The scale notes are all identical, but one octave higher in this position.

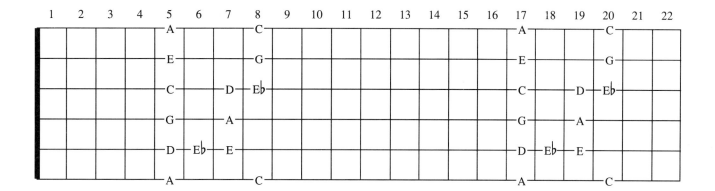

SECTION 3 - The Blue Scale, Pattern 2

You will need to visualize this pattern on your guitar fretboard, and in order to do this you must first practise playing the notes. The last two notes of the scale (G & A) are in the 3rd Blues scale pattern.

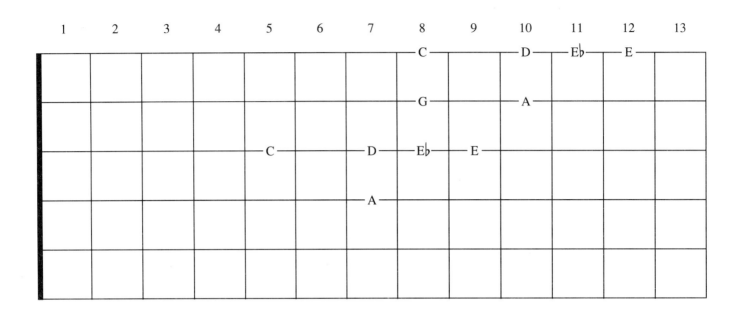

RIFF 31

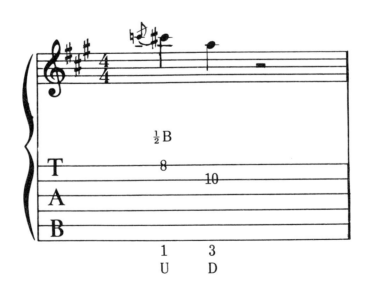

This is a frequently-played but simple riff. Play the ½ bend with an 'up' pick. You cannot *pull* the ½ bend because you are on the edge of the fretboard, so *push* the ½ bend into pitch with your 1st finger. Stop the bend with your plectrum once the pitch has been reached, then play the A with a 'down' pick, using vibrato to finish.

RIFF 32

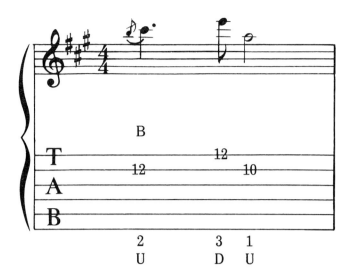

This is another extremely common riff. Play the bend with an 'up' pick. Keep the bend up while you hit the E with a 'down' pick, and finish with vibrato on the A. Add your 1st finger to assist the bend if necessary.

RIFF 33

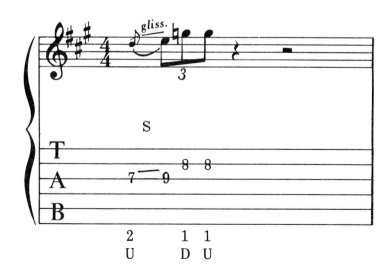

This riff is usually played in a rapid repeating sequence. Try playing the riff in groups of four times and eight times, stopping the last note with your plectrum for a muted effect.

RIFF 34

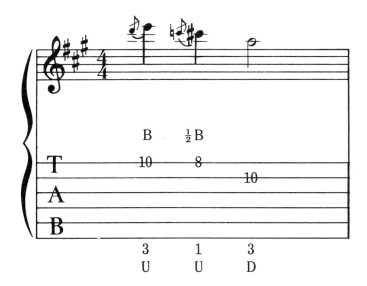

Start the riff with a tone bend. Stop the bend with your plectrum once the E is reached, then finish as you did in Riff 31.

RIFF 35

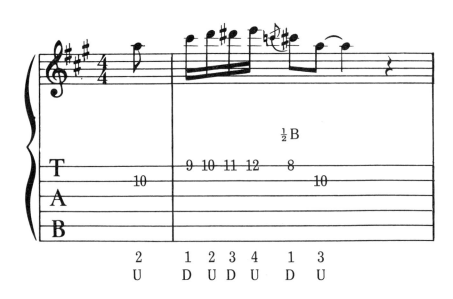

Start this riff with an 'up' pick on the A, then pick D-U-D-U on the chromatic run, finishing with D-U on the last two notes. Again, the last two notes are the same as Riff 31.

RIFF 36

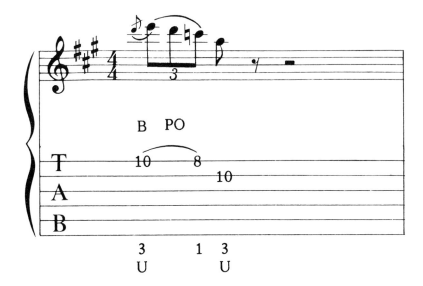

This riff is very similar to Riff 7. Use two 'up' picks and finish with vibrato. String bends sound better with 'up' picks because you can scrape up the string with the edge of your plectrum.

RIFF 37

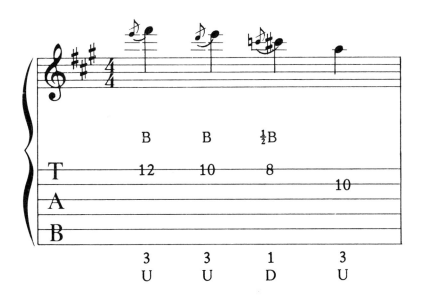

This riff is almost the same as Riff 34, except that you are starting with a tone bend at the 12th fret. Stop all bends with your plectrum once pitch is reached.

RIFF 38

This riff is exactly the same as Riff 26 but it is played in a different position on the fretboard. By studying riffs in this fashion you will be able to visualise the Blues scale patterns better. Many - but not all - of these riffs can be played in other areas of the guitar, in the same key. Most guitarists only play tone-bends on the three thinnest strings, so this makes some of the riffs which contain bends on more than one string impossible to play in other areas of the scale. Of course each riff can be played in the higher-register octave position.

RIFF 39

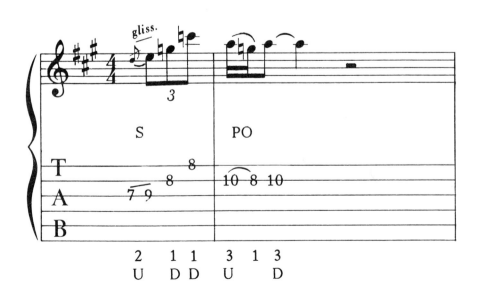

Play the opening slide with an 'up' pick. Use your 1st finger as a barre for the G & C notes. Pick 'up' for the pull-off and 'down' for the final A. Finish with vibrato.

RIFF 40

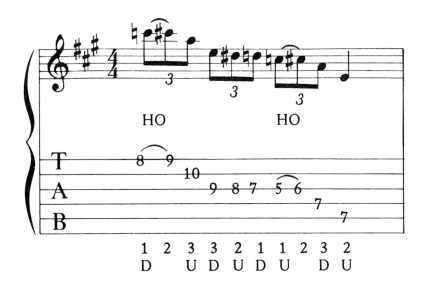

This is a good riff for finishing a Blues solo, but it can also be used for improvising - like any of the other riffs. Play the opening C with your 1st finger on the 8th fret 1st string, then hammer down your 2nd finger to produce the second note at the 9th fret 1st string. Then repeat the action on the 5th fret 3rd string.

RIFF 41

Play the slide with an 'up' pick, then the A with a 'down' pick. Play the bend with an 'up' pick. Once pitch has been reached, stop the bend with your plectrum. Finish with vibrato on the A.

RIFF 42

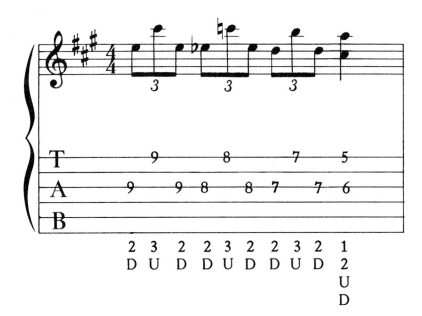

This riff involves using the 2nd finger of your right hand together with your plectrum. Hold your plectrum with your thumb and 1st finger and use this to play each of the 3rd string notes with 'down' picks, and all of the 1st string notes with your 2nd right-hand finger, plucking the string upwards. Play the last two notes together, with a squeezing action, picking 'down' and plucking 'up' at the same time.

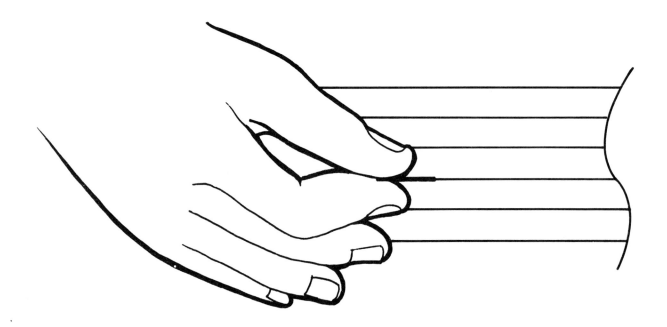

The Pick and Finger Technique

RIFF 43

This riff starts with the double pull-off technique using a 'down' pick. Then pick U-D for the F# and A. Finish with an 'up' pick on the bend and a 'down' pick on the E. Keep the bend up so both notes harmonize and fade together.

RIFF 44

This riff uses a pedal tone. This simply means the melody returns repeatedly to the same note, which in this case is A. Finish with vibrato.

RIFF 45

This is a simple but effective riff. Finish with vibrato.

RIFF 46

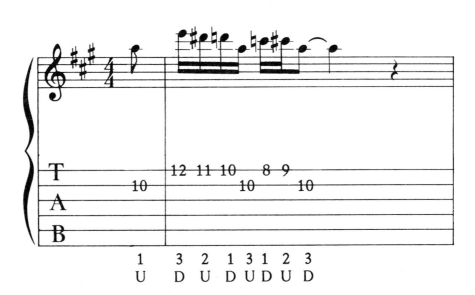

This riff sounds great when played fast. Use fast alternate picking, then finish with vibrato. For extra speed try turning your plectrum at an angle so you slice across the strings.

RIFF 47

Learning lots of riffs is the only sure way of ultimately being able to improvise Blues solos. If you simply play up and down the Blues scale with no added techniques or chromatic notes for colour and flavour, then your solos will sound uninteresting and plain.

RIFF 48

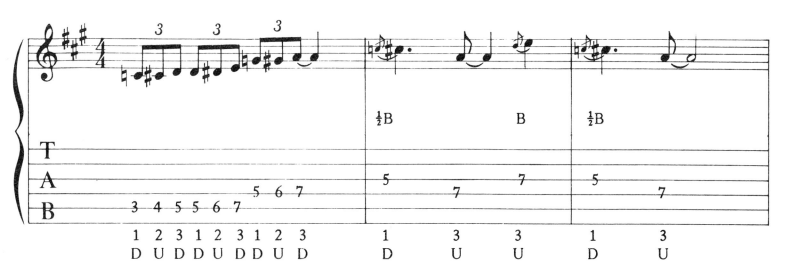

This riff is a good example of how to link riffs together. If you do this, however, you cannot use vibrato at the end of each riff or you will upset the musical flow. Common sense and listening to what you are playing will help you to develop musical continuity. The riff opens with the same notes as Riff 10.

RIFF 49

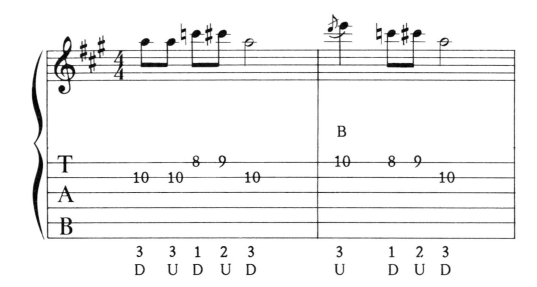

This riff is fairly simple to play. Stop the bend with your plectrum once you reach the E. Repeating the key note (A) is a technique used frequently by B B King.

RIFF 50

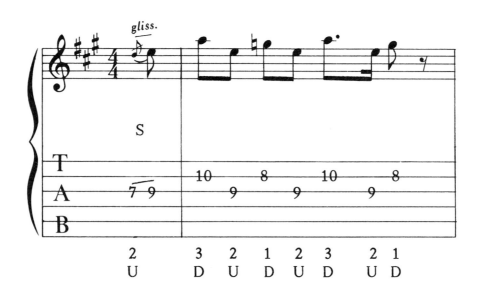

This is a very good riff to play several times in quick succession. Use U-D picking to keep your plectrum in between the strings. When repeating the riff, keep your fingers in place and leave out the slide.

HIGH REGISTER PLAYING

41

Some of the riffs we have just covered in the 2nd Blues Scale Pattern can also be played in the octave position - in this instance the extreme high register in the key of A. How easy this is to achieve really depends on your guitar fretboard access and the amount of frets on your guitar. On some guitars like the Les Paul or semi-acoustic models, you will probably have to bring your thumb around the front of the guitar to play these high-register riffs.

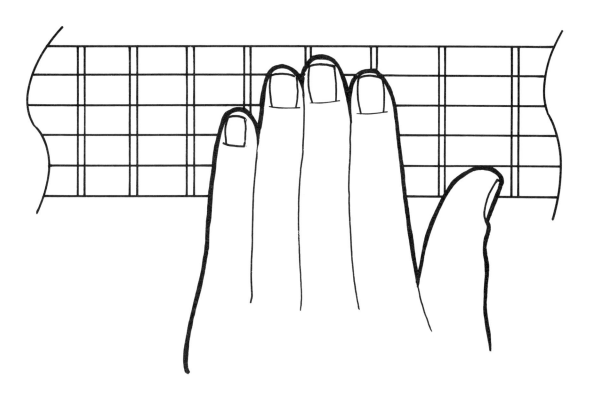

SECTION 4 - The Blues Scale, Pattern 3

This is the 3rd pattern of the Blues scale in A. As before, it is simply the same six notes - A C D E♭ E G A - in a different position on the fretboard.

```
    9      10     11     12     13     14     15     16     17
                                                G            A
                                C              D     E♭     E
                         G              A
                  C             D      E♭      E
                                A
```

RIFF 51

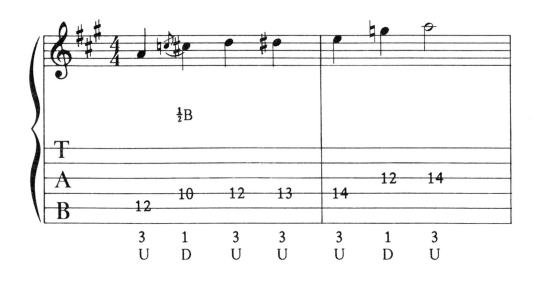

This is the same as Riff 1, but one octave higher. Again it is simply the Blues scale played with the semitone bend on the C. Try scraping your plectrum up the string on those consecutive 'up' picks, to create a staccato sound.

RIFF 52

This is another riff which uses a string rake. Use your 1st finger as a barre then slice your plectrum across the three strings, immediately taking the weight off the strings to mute the sound. Play the three-note chromatic run with U-D-U picking then play the bend with an 'up' pick. You can stop the bend with your plectrum or let it fade out. Play the last note with a 'down' pick and vibrato.

RIFF 53

Here is another 'repeat riff'. Keep the bend raised until you have played the E. Try repeating the riff in groups of four times, using U-D picking.

RIFF 54

With this riff you could repeat the first two notes a number of times before finishing with the semitone bend. Let the tone bend hang on, to harmonize with the G. The semitone bend can be played by pushing or pulling the string - decide for yourself which way feels the best. Don't forget to stop the semitone bend with your plectrum once pitch has been reached, and release the bend silently.

RIFF 55

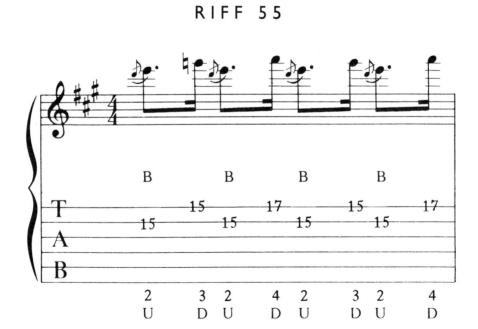

Push the bend up one tone, immediately playing the G while the bend is still raised. Repeat the bend and then play the A while the bend is still raised.

RIFF 56

Repeat the combined bend and pull-off, then switch fingers for the last bend. Add your 1st finger to assist the bend if necessary. Finish with vibrato.

RIFF 57

Play the double pull-off. Stop both bends with your plectrum once pitch has been reached and finish with vibrato on the A.

RIFF 58

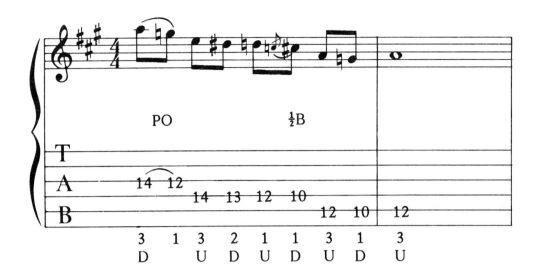

This riff consists of the Blues scale played in reverse. It should be fairly easy to play once you have learnt all the previous riffs. Stop the semitone bend with your plectrum as usual, and finish with vibrato.

RIFF 59

This is a fairly long riff containing most of the two octave Blues scale notes. Play the tone bend, then simply pick the string again while the bend is still raised.

RIFF 60

This is a fairly straightforward riff. Try to stick to the recommended fingering for the two pull-offs, and finish with vibrato.

RIFF 61

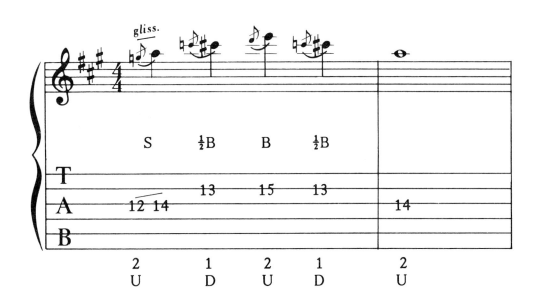

This riff is also fairly straightforward. Stop all bends with your plectrum once pitch is reached. Once again decide for yourself which is the easiest way to play the semitone bend - by pushing or pulling.

RIFF 62

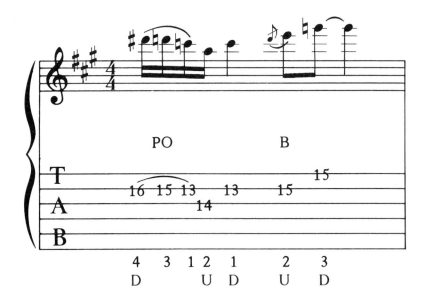

The double pull-off is slightly more difficult in the 13th position; otherwise this riff should be no real problem to you.

RIFF 63

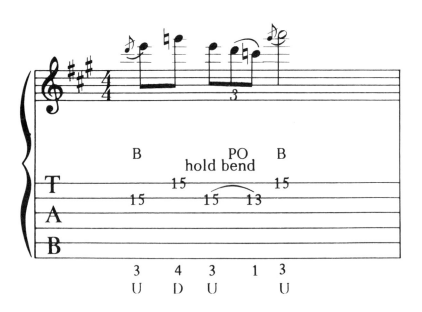

This riff is not as easy as it looks! Start by pushing the bend with your 3rd finger then play the G with your 4th finger, but keep the bend up while adding your 1st finger to the C, 13th fret 2nd string. Then release the bend to produce the pull-off, and finish with the E string bend. Use vibrato on the last bend, though you may find this difficult.

RIFF 64

This riff contains a tension-building chromatic run which resolves on the last two notes. Try to play the run fast, and finish with vibrato.

RIFF 65

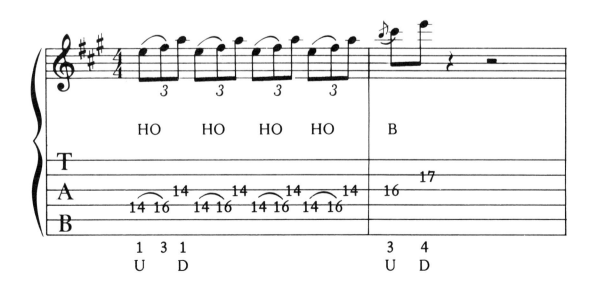

Hold down the two 14th fret notes with a 1st finger barre, then hammer-on the 3rd finger to the F#. Play the bend and keep it raised until you've played the E, so both notes harmonize and fade together.

RIFF 66

This riff should not give you any problems if you stick to the recommended picking. Don't forget to roll the 3rd finger down for the A & D notes (12th fret).

RIFF 67

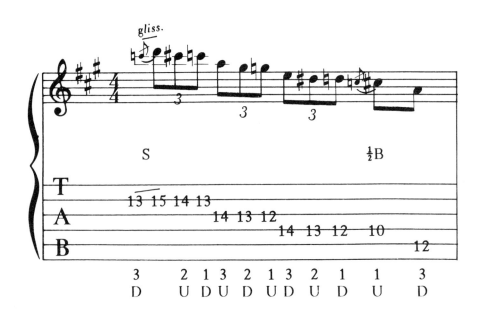

This is a descending chromatic-type Blues riff. The riff should give you no problems. Try to play it quickly, pausing only on the $1/2$ bend. Use vibrato on the last note.

RIFF 68

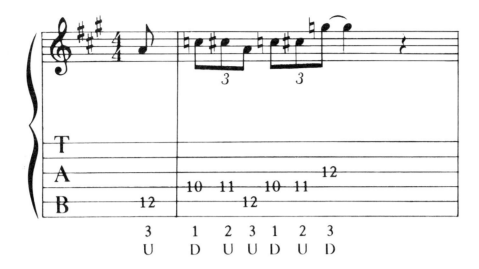

This is a straightforward note riff using no techniques. This should be easy compared with some of the riffs we have studied.

RIFF 69

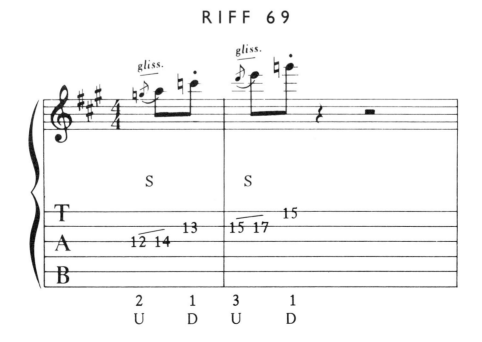

This is a short riff containing two slides. Play the third and the last note staccato.

RIFF 70

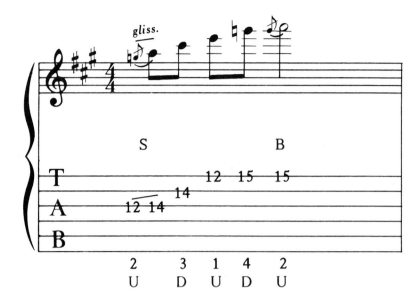

Here is a nice A7 arpeggio riff to finish on. Try using vibrato on the bend and letting the sound fade out.

SECTION 5 - Blues Chords

THE 12 BAR RIFF

The 12 Bar Blues chord progression is probably the most common and popular backing track ever recorded. Thousands of songs have been recorded using this basic rhythm part. Bands like Status Quo, The Blues Band, Chuck Berry, Eric Clapton Steve Gibbons, David Essex - there's too many to mention - have all used this versatile chord sequence. When you consider almost every Rock 'n' Roll and Blues track ever recorded is based on this progression, it highlights the importance of being able to play the 12 BAR BLUES.

The first rhythm guitar part you need to learn is the 12 BAR RIFF. As the name implies, this part is based on twelve bars of music.

Place your 1st finger as indicated below onto the 6th string 5th fret and your 3rd finger onto the 5th string 7th fret. You are going to play these two strings with four 'down' strums. Hit both strings with your plectrum twice, using a 'down' pick, thus making both strings sound at the same time. Playing two notes is called a double stop. Then on the 3rd strum put your 4th finger onto the 9th fret 5th string. Keep the 1st & 3rd fingers in position while reaching out for the F# with your 4th finger. For the 4th strum take away the 4th finger. It's quite a stretch isn't it?

Practise this riff until you can play it eight consecutive times. If you find the timing of the riff difficult, then count one-a-and-a; a syllable for each strum.

For the 2nd riff count two-a-and-a.
For the 3rd riff count three-a-and-a.
And so on.

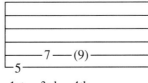

1st   3rd   4th

When you can play the riff eight times without stopping you are ready to shift the riff to the other fretboard positions.

So, play the riff:

8 times on A, 5th fret (the position you have just practised).

4 times on D, 10th fret.

4 times on A, 5th fret.

2 times on E, 12th fret.

2 times on D, 10th fret.

2 times on A, 5th fret.

Then finish with three 'down' strums on the E7 chord played at the 12th fret.

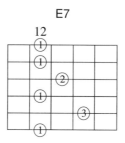

Now play the riffs again using this bar structure - two riffs per bar (each 'slash mark' represents one beat).

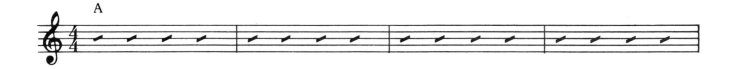

CHORDS AND THEIR ROOT NOTES

The root note of a chord is the note from which the chord is named. The root of A7 is A; the root of D7 is D, etc. For guitarists, a system of indicating which string plays the root of the chord has been devised. So, a Root 6 chord indicates that the root of the chord is played on the 6th string; r5 indicates the 5th string; r4 the 4th string, and so on.

x = Don't play

Now look at these four A7 chords.

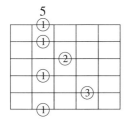 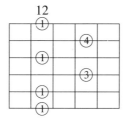 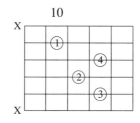 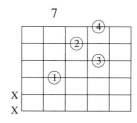

Each chord is a different pattern, made up of the same four notes - A, C#, E, G. This is because the 'formula' of A7 is:

1	3	5	♭7
A	C#	E	G

Basically the numbers 1 3 5 ♭7 are scale degrees taken from the altered A major scale. The notes of the A major scale are as follows:

A	B	C#	D	E	F#	G#
1	2	3	4	5	6	7

CONSTRUCTING DOMINANT - TYPE CHORDS

To construct 7th chords, the 7th scale degree is flattened one fret from G# to G♮. The scale we are then left with is:

A	B	C#	D	E	F#	G♮
1	2	3	4	5	6	♭7

Here is the major scale in two octaves (played twice through):

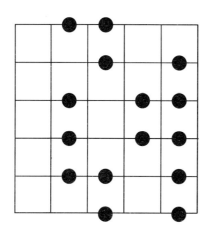

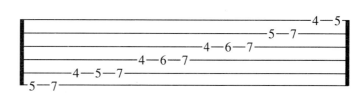

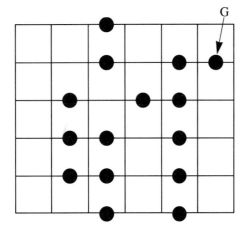

Now play the 'altered' major scale. Notice the pattern has changed slightly. This is to allow you to play the second G at the 8th fret 2nd string instead of at the 3rd fret 1st string. The latter would have been out of position.

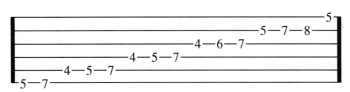

THE NOTES OF THE BLUES CHORD

A7	=	1 3 5 ♭7 A C# E G
A7sus4	=	1 4 5 ♭7 A D E G
A7⁻5	=	1 3 ⁻5 ♭7 A C# E♭ G
A7⁺5	=	1 3 ⁺5 ♭7 A C# E# G
A9	=	1 3 5 ♭7 9 A C# E G B
A7⁺9	=	1 3 5 ♭7 ⁺9 A C# E G B#
A7⁻5⁺9	=	1 3 ⁻5 ♭7 ⁺9 A C# E♭ G B#
A7⁺5⁻9	=	1 3 ⁺5 ♭7 ⁻9 A C# E# G B♭
A7⁺5⁺9	=	1 3 ⁺5 ♭7 ⁺9 A C# E# G B#
A7⁻5⁻9	=	1 3 ⁻5 ♭7 ⁻9 A C# E♭ G B♭
A11	=	1 3 5 ♭7 9 11 A C# E G B D
A13	=	1 3 5 ♭7 9 11 13 A C# E G B D F#
A13⁻9	=	1 3 5 ♭7 ⁻9 11 13 A C# E G B♭ D F#

In the terminology used for this book, the minus sign (-) means ♭ and the plus sign (+) means #.

Note: Technically the +5 is always E#, although most guitar players will simply call it F. Similarly, the +9 should be called B#, although most guitar players will call it C.

These 'altered' chords, as they are known, are very common in Jazz and Big Band playing, but for playing over the 12 bar riff in a Rock 'n' Roll or Blues Band the most effective chords are:

A7

A7+9

A9

A13

You can play any of these chords while the rhythm guitar player is playing the 12 bar riff on A, and the sound of the Blues chords will blend well together. When the rhythm player changes to D, you can use any D-type chord from these four choices; and when the rhythm player changes to E, the same applies. You can also mix them up, for example:

The 12 bar riff	Example 1	Example 2
A x 8	A7 x 8	A13 x 8
D x 4	D9 x 4	D13 x 4
A x 4	A13 x 4	A9 x 4
E x 2	E7 + 9 x 2	E7 x 2
D x 2	D7 + 9 x 2	D7 x 2
A x 2	A7 x 2	A7 + 9 x 2
Finish on E7	Finish on E9	Finish on E13

To reduce fretboard movement when changing chords we need to learn at least two positions of each pattern - an *r6 pattern* and an *r5 pattern*.

Now make a recording of the 12 bar riff, and play the three 7th chord patterns over it.

USING DOMINANT 7th - TYPE CHORDS

Play the r6 at the 5th fret = A7

Play the r5 at the 5th fret = D7

Play the r2 at the 5th fret = E7

You may find the timing awkward at first, so experiment with it. Obviously if you just play these chords alone, there will be no timing problem - it's fitting these chords in with the 12 bar riff that takes a bit of practice. Record about 5 - 10 minutes and try to play some of the seventy riffs over your recorded backing track.

12 bar riff using 7th chords

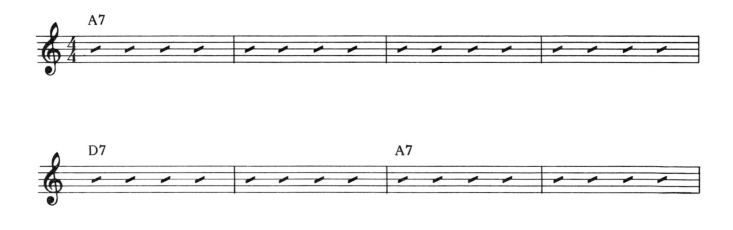

The 12 Bar riff progression ended on E7 12th fret. You can actually use any E7 type chord to finish this progression, e.g.

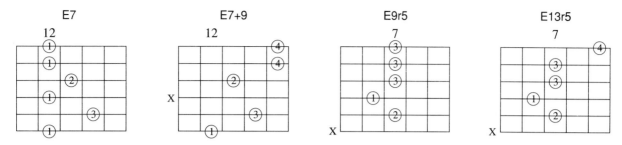

You can also use any of the other altered chords (but these four sound the best). The E7+9 r5 sounds really good:

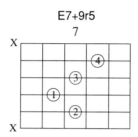

Try adding vibrato to the final chord as you finish the riff, (but you will find this difficult).

MIXING UP DOMINANT - TYPE CHORDS

The next example involves mixing up these 7th chord patterns:

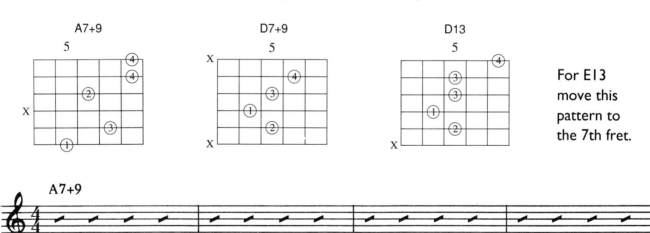

For E13 move this pattern to the 7th fret.

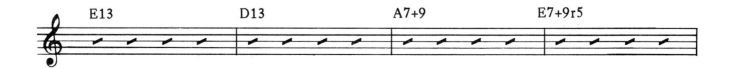

USING DOMINANT 9th - TYPE CHORDS

Here's another Blues chord progression using 9th chords. On the r6 version I am leaving off the bass notes (6th & 5th strings) in order to make the chord easier to play, and to produce a brighter sound. The r5 pattern sounds OK without removing any notes. Try sliding the chords for a nice effect. Do this by sliding from the fret below, such as A♭9 to A9; D♭9 to D9, etc.

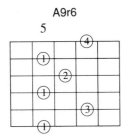
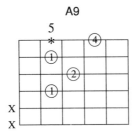
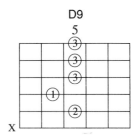

Technically, the second chord is no longer a r6 since the 6th string is not present. We are only learning this root note system as an aid to identifying chords. As there is no root note in this chord we shall call it an 'assumed' root I chord. You now have a home base through which to identify this similar pattern in other keys. The large asterisk on the (thinnest) E string is the assumed root note.

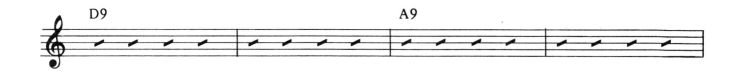

Try to be inventive with your Blues chord rhythm parts, and use:
* Off beat rhythms
* Slides
* Emphasis on the high notes of the chords
* Inversions

THE MINOR BLUES

For the minor Blues most of the seventy riffs will still sound great, but we cannot use the 1/2 bend techniques because this technique is designed to fit only with the 3rd degree (C#) of the A major chord.

The 3rd degree of the A minor chord is C, (A minor triad = A C E) so you must leave out the semitone bend and play this note straight.

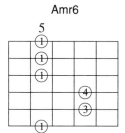
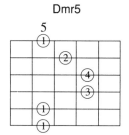
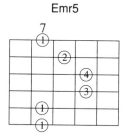

If you decide to record a demo tape or are lucky enough to play on a recording, then work out your solos note for note, analysing the chords you are playing over.

Wrong notes only sound wrong if you stop or hang on to them too long! If you are planning a solo and you decide to pause while playing a bend or sustaining a note, make sure that the note you choose is in the underlying harmony.

Most guitarists while improvising with Blues riffs hit dodgy notes at times, but an experienced player can disguise them by 'sliding'.

When you are checking the notes contained in a chord for soloing over don't rely on the formula, because some chord patterns do not contain every note. Instead look at the actual chord pattern you are recording and break this chord down into notes.

CHORD SUBSTITUTION

Look at bar 2 in the example below. Usually in the 12 bar Blues the first four bars are all A-type chords. The Eb7+9 is actually a substitution chord based on 'common tones'. This means I have used a similarly-structured chord to enhance the harmonic feel of this progression.

A7   = A   C#   E   G
Eb7+9 = Eb   G   Bb   Db   F#

Common tones means 'notes in common' (the same notes).

The A7 contains C# & G.
The Eb7+9 contains Db (same notes as C# & G).
These are common tones.

In bar 4 the Em7 chord is also a substitute chord for the A7.
Em7 = E   G   B   D
A7 = A   C#   E   G

Two common tones - E & G.

Some guitarists use substitution chords with only one common tone. This depends on how it sounds - your ear is always the final judge.

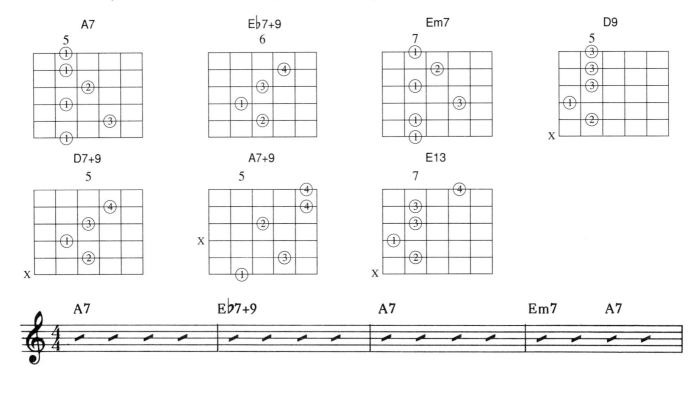

In the next example notice the use of substitution chords once again.

A7 = A C# E G

A7-9 = A C# E G B♭

C# diminished 7 = C# E G B♭

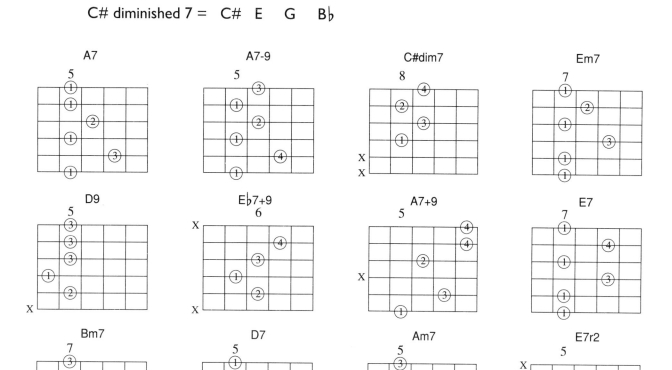

Because you are now learning Jazz/Blues progressions you will have to be more selective when adding riffs to harmonic progressions. Most players do this by analysing a progression, trying out ideas to see if they work, and working out lead guitar passages, always aiming for a 'smooth ending'.

JAZZ/BLUES PASSING CHORDS

While playing Blues chord exercises try to produce your own rhythm variations. The main objective is to keep in time. Tap your foot and keep the pace regular. If you have trouble tapping your foot and playing at the same time, use a metronome or a drum machine.

Notice that the difference between the A9, A9+5 & A13 chord patterns is only slight. One note is changing each time. These passing chord patterns are very common in Jazz Blues chord progressions.

Notice the A9, A9+5 & A13 chords do not contain the root note. The large asterisk on the 1st (thinnest) E string is where the assumed root note would be. Each small **x** at the side of a chord indicates strings not to be played.

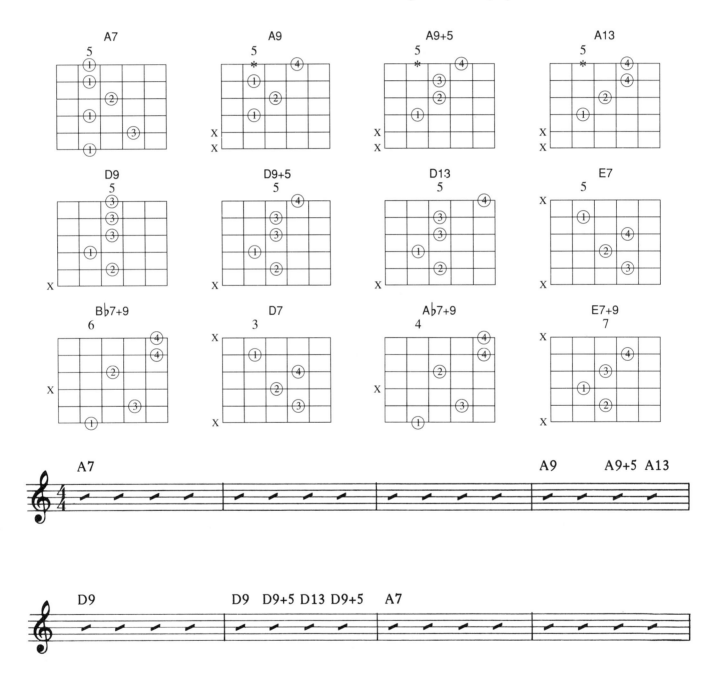

SECTION 6 - Chord Index

CHORD TITLES

Note: Chord symbols should be as short as possible to enable guitarists to interpret them quickly. The other titles I have given to some chords are rare but show that arrangers' styles vary.

A7 + 5

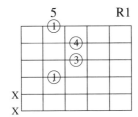

Other titles used:
Aug 7
A7 +

Formula: 1   3   +5   b7
          A   C# E#   G

A lot of altered chord patterns are played on the treble strings only, leaving out the bass notes.

A7 - 5

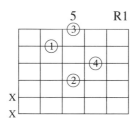
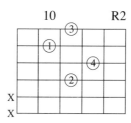

Other titles used:
Dom 7b5

Formula: 1   3   -5   b7
          A   C# Eb   G

Notice how the chord shapes are identical in the above patterns, but the notes are in a different order.

A9 - 5

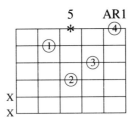 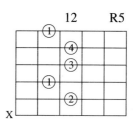

Other titles used:
9 Dim 5
Aug 11

Formula: I   3   -5   b7   9
          A   C# Eb   G   B

Augmented 11 = #4th. This is because the 4th & 11th degrees of the 'altered' A scale are the same note - D. Sharpen D and you have D#. The flattened 5th degree of the scale is Eb.

D# & Eb are the same note, so some players call this chord the Aug 11th.

A7 + 5 - 9

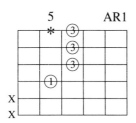 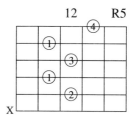

Other titles used:
7#5b9

Formula: I   3   +5   b7   -9
          A   C# E#   G   Bb
              (F♮)

It's only by studying chords and analysing the tones not present in a chord that you can really start to understand chord theory.

A7-9

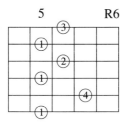

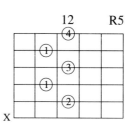

Other titles used:
7♭9

Formula: 1   3   5   ♭7   -9
          A   C#   E   G   B♭

A9+5

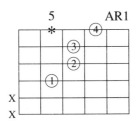

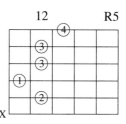

Other titles used:
9#5
9 Aug

Formula: 1   3   +5   ♭7   9
          A   C#   E#   G   B
                    (F♮)

The many variations of these chords are confusing, so you must memorize them all.

A7-5-9

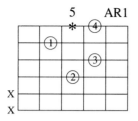
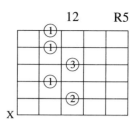

Formula: 1   3   -5   b7   -9
          A   C# Eb   G   Bb

A11

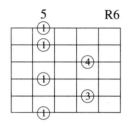
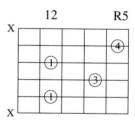

Formula: 1   3   5   b7   9   11
          A   C# E   G   B   D

When you analyse this chord you will notice that neither pattern contains the 3rd (C#). Technically, a 3rd is present in the formula, but most guitar 11th chord patterns do not contain the 3rd. The only place where we could play the 3rd on the above r6 pattern is at the 8th fret on the 6th or 1st string. The 3rd in both of these places would not sound very good. The 3rd needs to be played on the inside strings (2nd, 3rd & 4th) to sound in balance and stabilize the chord.

A7 - 5 + 9

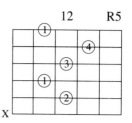

Other titles used:
7♭5#9

Formula: 1   3   -5   ♭7   +9
          A   C#   Eb   G   B#
                                         (C)

Please note some of these chords played at the 12th fret may be difficult to finger in that position. But the object is to show you the pattern so you can apply it to other keys. If we were playing in A, we would use the r6 or r1 because these chord patterns lie in a more accessible area.

A7 + 5 + 9

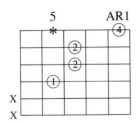 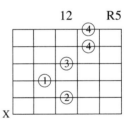

Other titles used:
7#5#9

Formula: 1   3   +5   ♭7   +9
          A   C#   E#   G   B#
                         (F♮)   (C♮)

A7 sus 4

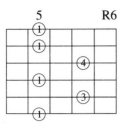
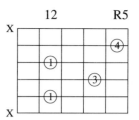

Other titles used:
7 sus

Formula: 1   4   5   b7
            A   D   E   G

Notice the 3rd has been replaced by the 4th. The reason we can use these same patterns for 11th and sus 4ths is because the 11th degree D is the same note as the 4th degree D. The 11th is simply one octave higher. Even though the 11th chord formula contains six notes, there are only four notes present in both patterns: the same four notes as in the sus 4 formula - A D E G.

A13 - 9

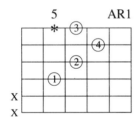
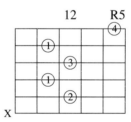

Other titles used:
13b9

Formula: 1   3   5   b7   -9   11   13
            A   C#   E   G   Bb   D   F#

If you are having difficulty producing five clear notes with the r5 pattern, omit the 5th string (A) note. This is quite common.

CHORDS WITH NOTES MISSING FROM THE FORMULAS

Very often chords may not contain every note of the formula because it is not always possible to play them all at the same time. For example, take a chord such as A13♭9.

The formula for this chord is:

1	3	5	♭7	♭9	11	13
A	C#	E	G	B♭	D	F#

Seven notes - but only six strings on your guitar, so something has to go. The most important notes in a chord are:

(a) The 3rd - this determines if the chord is major or minor.

(b) The notes which give the chord its name, for example if it's a ninth chord, the 9th.

(c) The 7th - in any chord 'above' A7, such as A9, A11, A13 (or any altered version of these chords).

(d) The root

But, with regard to (d) - the root note may be omitted. This seems illogical but it is quite common in altered chords.

When planning a worked-out solo, always analyse each chord pattern to see exactly which notes are present in the chords. This way you will not include notes in the solo which have been left out of the chords.

The best way to study chords is to take each formula and look at every inversion of that chord to familiarize yourself with the position of each chord degree in each pattern.

Note: altered chords are sometimes called 'extended chords' or 'extensions'.